HOPE LIVES HERE

Covering the City in Prayer for 30 Days and Beyond

Copyright © Dawn Walda 2023
Published by Dawn Walda
Windsor, Ontario

All rights reserved. This book is protected by the copyright laws of Canada. No part of this publication may be reproduced, stored in a retrieval system, or transmitted in any form or by any means—electronic, mechanical, photocopy, recording or any other—except for brief quotations, without prior permission of the author.

Scripture quotations marked KJV are taken from the Holy Bible, King James Version (Public Domain).

Scripture quotations marked ASV are taken from the Holy Bible, American Standard Version (Public Domain).

Scripture quotations marked NKJV are from the New King James Version®. Copyright © 1982 by Thomas Nelson, Inc. Used by permission. All rights reserved.

Scripture quotations marked NIV® are from the New International Version®. Copyright © 1973, 1978, 1984, 2011 by Biblica, Inc.™ Used by permission. All rights reserved worldwide.

Scripture quotations marked ESV are from the ESV Bible® (The Holy Bible, English Standard Version®), copyright © 2001 by Crossway Bibles, a publishing ministry of Good News Publishers. Used by permission. All rights reserved. http://www.crossway.org

Scripture quotations marked NET are from the NET Bible® copyright ©1996, 2019 by Biblical Studies Press, L.L.C. http://netbible.com All rights reserved. Scripture quoted by permission.

Scripture quotations marked NASB are from the New American Standard Bible. Copyright © 1960, 1962, 1963, 1968, 1971, 1972, 1973, 1975, 1977 by the Lockman foundation. Used by permission.

Scripture quotations marked AMP are taken from The AMPLIFIED Bible, Copyright © 1954, 1958, 1962, 1964, 1965, 1987, 2015 by The Lockman Foundation. All rights reserved. Used by permission. (www.Lockman.org)

Scripture quotations marked NLT are taken from the Holy Bible, New Living Translation, copyright © 1996, 2004, 2007 by Tyndale House Foundation. Used by permission of Tyndale House Publishers, Inc., Carol Stream, Illinois 60188. All rights reserved. http://www.newlivingtranslation.com/ http://www.tyndale.com

Scripture quotations marked BSB are taken from The Holy Bible, Berean Study Bible, BSB. Copyright ©2016, 2018 by Bible Hub. Used by Permission. All Rights Reserved Worldwide. www.berean.bible

ISBN: 978-1-7390770-1-3

DEDICATION

"Until We Meet Again"

Three of my dear friends have had to utter these words at the funerals of their beloved children. The lives of their sons and daughter taken far too soon. The grip and stronghold of addiction strangling them. The final hold stealing them from their families, homes, churches, and streets. Far too many left in grief. But my friends' stories did not end here. How could they move on? They have Hope.
The hope of Jesus Christ.

I have had the privilege of seeing these three mommas rise in and with hope as they have found their strength in God, God's family, in their faith which has been immovable, unshakeable. Their faith journey giving testimony to our Beloved Jesus Who has been their source of strength. Their hope! In honour of these dear women, and their beloved children,

TIM, JOHN & ANGEL

I commit these writings and prayers to God so that He alone will be seen, declared, honoured, and glorified. Our cities coming together in prayerful agreement and declaring that Jesus Lives Here! Hope lives here!

TABLE OF CONTENTS

Dedication		3
Introduction		7
Hope Street		13
How Do We Begin?		15
I.	May My Life Be Your Love Song	17
	• Days 1-10	19-37
II.	May We Be Your Love Song	39
	• Days 11-20	43-69
	• No Other Love	55
III.	Jesus, You Are Our Love Song	71
	• Days 21-30	75-101
What's Next?		103
YESHUA (This is Our God)		105
Credits/Endnotes		106

INTRODUCTION

It was a cool Saturday morning that I drove down one of our busy city streets seeing the usual morning sights. People running to work, to catch the bus, running to the local coffee shop, others on their routine dog walk. There was something that caught my attention. It was certainly, "out of place." Unusual. It was dirty and would appear to most to be "useless." There at the intersection, my eyes were drawn to a very visibly dirty bed comforter piled on a park bench. Perhaps, it was once perfectly white and pristine, but there it was tattered, stained, yellowed. At the very next stoplight there was another park bench. It too had a comforter. This time, the comforter cocooned a young man whom I assumed had been nestled there all night. His blanket, just as stained and tattered as the first one. The cold park bench his solitary place. The morning traffic and people noise unheard.

As I drove away, my heart broke into song. I found myself surprised at my response as brokenness might seem to be the more appropriate and immediate response. I admit, that was wrapped up in my feelings, but out of that drive by, my heart began to sing with the idea of Holy Spirit, the Comforter, covering the city. Love calling to my city in chaos, with the glorious beauty of Holy Spirit hovering. Mightily at work. Genesis 1:2 NIV says, "Now the earth was formless and empty, darkness was over the surface of the deep, and the Spirit of God was hovering over the waters." What beautiful imagery this was for me. The glorious truth of Holy Spirit's work despite what I was seeing. All this culminating in an anthem. An anthem? Yes! "Love Calling." The whispering in the wind calling the city to rise in faith, hope and love. The city blanketed by the Great Comforter, Holy Spirit.

I have lived in other cities, several in fact, and travelled to many more, and this "Love Calling" message resides over all of them. There is a desperation within all cities for those who are seeking answers, seeking Truth. The Holy Spirit's beckoning whisper blowing strongly through the streets. In the forgotten places and spaces. God's love song calling each one home—unto Himself.

Presently residing in Windsor, Ontario, I can see the ever-increasing needs within our city. So many lives taken captive by destructive behaviours—self-harm, depression, anxiety, alcohol, and drug abuse. Families, lives, businesses, all destroyed by the overcoming power of addiction, abuse and sadly overdose and death. Our first responders daily walking into and through the unimaginable. Their workplace, lives and families in turn affected by this ever-increasing crisis within and over our city. The need for the call of love ever increasing with intensity.

I began to ask myself what can I do? What am I already doing? Could I do more? What do I have to offer that would make an impact—citywide? The angst to do more has been increasing within me. Seeking the Lord in prayer, I began to ask the Lord what I could do. What is the biggest way that I can encourage all of us to see our city transformed in an expedited way? My offering growing exponentially, and the harvest requiring a "spiritual combine."

The Lord has called me to do many things in my lifetime. This part of my faith journey seems to have settled in 3 major components. First and foremost is my love for God; He is my life! He made me for Him, to love Him. I in no way have a crisis with my identity for I have come to know and love all that He has called me and called me to. Second, I have come to celebrate the use of words, especially the use of imagery in word. From humble beginnings in basic high school English, to now authoring my second book, I have come to love the use of words to help create a visual for you, my readers. You in turn, seeing my Beloved and learning more of Him and loving Him more day by day. Third has been the use of photos to compliment the word imagery. Something I have affectionately called, "photographizing." It has led me time and time again to slow down, see the unseen things and capture them in ways not seen by those who just rush by. It was this triple threat that led me to resolve in preparing this 30-day prayer book for my city, for your city, and our nation. This collaborative of scriptures, photos and devotional thoughts was created as a source of inspiration for all of us to unite our hearts in collective prayer for our hamlet, town, or city. All of us coming together in a prayer of agreement. An invitation to pray more, pray differently, pray more specifically. A collective standing to see the destruction of overdosing. To see abuse and its deadly pathways, completely overturned and undone. To see mental health healed and those suffering will find the rest, peace and sound mind they so desperately long for. To see families restored. Lives redeemed. Prodigal hearts turned toward home. Not just for my city, but "your" city and the cities all around us. Each and everyone joining in a prayer of agreement for the lost souls in our cities. So many lost and searching. We who are Christ followers have the most precious answer for them, our Beloved JESUS!

My prayer is that eyes would be opened wider to the great need within our cities. That our hearts, like mine, would be stirred to greater action through prayer, and love. And we, the Church, the Bride of Christ, would live out our faith and share the good news of the Gospel to everyone we meet. Sharing the love of Jesus—always. We the Church carry the greatest HOPE ever! And the result? Lives will find the person of Jesus and hope. I can already hear the laughter of children as they see mom and dad united in Jesus. I can hear fathers speaking life and love into their children. I can hear wives arising in their true beauty as they hear and know their identity in Christ. Husbands loving and celebrating their wives. Wives adoring, loving, and honoring their husbands. Everyone coming together in a unanimous victory shout; these miracles, signs and wonders are all from the hand of Jesus and Him alone.

I can hear this call to the Church for it is loud and clear! Your city is in crisis, and they need Jesus. Love is calling and beckoning those who are lost in sin. Jesus came to seek and save the lost. To set the captives free. To heal. To restore. To give sight to the blind. To give life in abundance. Would you join me in hearing, declaring, and praying this for my city? For your city? Can you hear the whisper in the wind? Love truly is calling both His Beloved, the Church, and to all found on the streets marked with Hope.

HOPE STREET

Hope walks alone on the street

Can anybody know her? Can anybody name her?

Praying for her soul to keep

Does Anybody see her? Can anybody hear her? Oh..., Oh...

There's a whisper in the wind

Can anybody hear it? Can anybody name it?

Singing songs of deliverance

Can anybody hear it? Can anybody sing it?

There is a Power we cannot see

Can anybody feel it? Can Anybody know it?

Holy Spirit's moving on our streets

We are under, under Your cover

Hope finds Faith in the night

Not alone now, Coming Home now

Together they set their fears to flight

Letting go now, being free now

This is Love, This is Love. Love Calling, Love Calling. This is Love,

This is Love Calling you home; You're not alone.

HOW DO WE BEGIN?

Let us begin by marking our calendars, paper or electronic, and settle into the most incredible 30 days of prayer. Coming with great expectancy. In/by faith seeing our city transformed. Every single day for 30 days and beyond. Our churches being filled with those whose lives have been transformed by the power of Jesus. Get yourselves and the church ready; they are coming!

May we begin by believing in faith that our God is going to do some amazing things over the next 30 days. For what we are about to embark on I believe will not only change your life, but your family, home, work, church and beyond. As Paul wrote, "therefore, I urge you, brothers and sisters, by the mercies of God, to present your bodies (dedicating all of yourselves, set apart) as a living sacrifice, holy and well-pleasing to God, which is your rational (logical, intelligent) act of worship" (Romans 12:1 AMP). May our joining in prayer and declaring the word of God over us, the Church, and our beloved cities be sweet. Believing for exponential growth and a monumental harvest. Lord of the harvest, even now!

May we pause for a moment to reflect on this 30-day prayer. Prayerfully considering our level of commitment. Taking into consideration how much time we want to invest and what size our return will be. Do you even see our city in crisis? May the following prayers lead us all to further knowing, going, doing, and seeing.

Lord, may I be open to all that You have for me. May I even now inquire of You as to what part I may play in the answers that I am seeking for through the next 30 days of prayer. I commit to You in obedience all that You would have for me. I am excitedly expectant. Lord may my life be Your love song. Walking in surrendered obedience. Abiding in the Vine—Jesus. If there be anything in me that You desire to work on, deal with, I offer myself as a living sacrifice. Your compassionate heart gifting me repentance. I accept such a beautiful and ansformative gift. Receive Your healing, forgiveness, and restoration, transformation. With my heart, mouth and life declaring I belong to You and You, alone. Now and forevermore. I pray all this in the name of Jesus, Amen!

Let's go, Church! I believe God has some incredible answers to prayer for each of us, for the Church and for our city. I have seen Him in multiple ways in just putting this book together and I know that which He has planned will be completed. There is much to be done and many of us to do it! The Lord is calling us out, calling us up, calling us into. It's time! It's time! It's time Church to rise up in our overcoming victory through Christ Jesus and Him alone and loudly declaring that JESUS IS LORD!

MAY MY LIFE BE YOUR LOVE SONG

Days 1-10

Day 1

I pray that your hearts will be flooded with light so that you can understand the confident hope He has given to those He called—His holy people who are his rich and glorious inheritance (Ephesians 1:18 NLT, emphasis mine).

Oh Lord, what beauty is found in my knowing of Your confident hope. The understanding of the finished work of Jesus. In and through all that You have done for me, I am declared Holy. My inheritance glorious. Beautiful. May my prayer today be that You will increase my understanding. No longer just knowing of You but "knowing" You. May I be one who lives "in the shelter of the Most High (who) finds rest in the shadow of the Almighty. This I declare about the LORD: He alone is my refuge, my place of safety; He is my God, and I trust Him" (Psalm 91:1-2 NLT).

You alone are my refuge. My safe place. You are my God. In no other one do I put my trust. For I shall have no other gods before You. May my life today be lived from this glorious knowing. May I be reminded today of my confident hope who is Jesus! Thank you, Jesus, for the finished work of Your cross. I count it both an honour and privilege to serve You and Your beloved city today.

May the Light of Christ be evident in and through me. I pray all of this in the mighty name of Jesus. - so be it!

Day 2

For You are my hope, O Lord GOD; You are my trust from my youth. By You I have been upheld from birth; You are He who took me out of my mother's womb. My praise shall be continually of You. I have become as a wonder to many, but You are my strong refuge. Let my mouth be filled with Your praise and with Your glory all the day (Psalm 71:5-8 NKJV).

Oh Lord, how precious is our hope, in YOU! You have been faithful for years. Always supplying all my needs according to Your provisional hands. Your heart filled with love and affection for me. Leading me always in paths of righteousness for Your glory and Yours alone. I have always been wanted, known, desired by You. Known in my mother's womb. In this incredible knowing, the sustaining power of Your provisional faithful hands, I can and must sing praises continually. Putting off the spirit of heaviness and donning the garment of praise—always! I will speak of Your greatness—always! I will declare Your incredible safekeeping—always! I will daily speak of Your great love and affection for me. For I was made by Love, in love, to be loved, to become love. May I treasure this understanding—always! I pray all this in the mighty name of Jesus. - so be it!

Day 3

For I know what I have planned for you,' says the Lord. I have plans to prosper you, not to harm you. I have plans to give you a future filled with hope (Jeremiah 29:11 NET).

    I rejoice and praise You Lord for the incredible plans that You alone have for me. No one else knowing all these incredible plans and purposes. My mouth declaring that You alone God, know everything about me. All that You have for me is good and will see completion. These incredible plans are to prosper me and never to harm me. For I am always and evermore protected in and through Your faithful, loving, and caring hands. Your plans include my future, and it is filled with hope. No one or nothing can tell me what is before me, for You alone have all things written for me. Your words over me are great, powerful and will see completion. So, thank you Lord for Your amazing plans, purposes, and provision to see every single ordered "next step" to completion. I pray all this in the mighty name of Jesus. - so be it!

Day 4

May the God of hope fill you with all joy and peace in believing [through the experience of your faith] that by the power of the Holy Spirit you will abound in hope and overflow with confidence in His promises (Romans 15:13 AMP).

May Your hope fill me Lord with all joy and peace. May I not be focused on me and my desires, but steadfastly focused on You. For all joy and peace is found in You and You alone. Increase my faith. May I not be focused on the depths of my unbelief but increase and grow my mustard seed faith. May it grow, mature and flourish. Abundant harvest through Your Holy Spirit in me. Teaching me, instructing me, and empowering me to walk in confident trust as Abraham did believing for the fulfillment of the promise You gave him (Romans 4). May I never be caught off guard focusing on doubt or be taken by disbelief but anchored in confident trust of Your faithfulness—always! I praise and glorify You, Lord! I pray all of this in the mighty name of Jesus. - so be it!

Day 5

I wait for the LORD, my soul waits, And in His word I do hope (Psalm 130:5 NKJV).

Lord, I know that all my steps are ordered and purposed. Your plans perfectly given and orchestrated by You, for me. May I know and accept that "waiting" is part of Your steps. You do not waste these precious moments nor are they a waste of my time. For the "process," the space between the asking and the receiving is never wasted by You. I trust Your heart in the process. I learn much there. For You will never invest without an incredible return. May I always remain focused on the truths of Your Words that have declared that You "will" supply ALL my needs. Each one. May I cherish Your Holy Word, the Bible. May I spend time daily in the Word. May I allow the Word to work in and through me. Always teaching me. Transforming me. Showing me. Always and ever expectant to receive. May I delight in the waiting. May I delight in the waiting, Lord. For it's in the waiting, that You are with me. In the beside still water moments that I am refreshed and restored. We are drawn together in the sweet place of abiding and I can say and declare, in the waiting, "it is well with my soul." I pray all of this in the mighty name of Jesus. - so be it!

Day 6

But now, thus says the LORD, who created you, O Jacob, And He who formed you, O Israel: "Fear not, for I have redeemed you; I have called you by your name; You are Mine. When you pass through the waters, I will be with you; And through the rivers, they shall not overflow you. When you walk through the fire, you shall not be burned, nor shall the flame scorch you (Isaiah 43:1-2 NKJV).

What a glorious encouragement and truth You have declared and given to me to "fear not!" My heart and mind assured of Your intentional purposes for me. The assurance of knowing that You alone formed me. You have called me, and I am Yours. What a blessed place to abide. Your assurance of Your faithful presence—always. When I am passing through the waters and rivers seem overwhelming, I know full well that they will NOT overtake me. No weapon formed against me shall prosper (Isaiah 54:17). For You have given me all I need to be more than a conqueror (Romans 8:37) and this You declared me to be in Your Holy Word.

I am forevermore sheltered in Your loving sheltering wings. Therein I find all the safety, strength, and peace I need—daily! For there is never a time where You are not at work in my life. Nor is there ever a time where You do not think of me. For I am held near and dear to Your heart. May I daily hold You close to my heart as well. My heart praying Colossians 1:23 (KJV), "if (I) continue in the faith grounded and settled and be not moved away from the hope of the gospel." Teach me to remain. Teach me to abide. For there is no other place I would rather be than near the heart of God. Hearing His love story over me. The great joy and delight He takes in those who seek You. They will always find You. I give You thanks and praise for Your never-failing love for me. I cannot help but give You my life, living a life worthy of the calling. Today, I love You. Today, I trust You. Today, my hope is in You. I pray all of this in the mighty name of Jesus. - so be it!

Day 7

Therefore, if you have been raised with Christ, keep seeking the things that are above, where Christ is, seated at the right hand of God. Set your minds on the things that are above, not on the things that are on earth (Colossians 3:1-2 NASB).

How good it is, the knowledge of my standing with God. That in my being raised with Christ, I have a blessed hope. I am ever mindful to set my mind on You and You alone. I pray Holy Spirit to continue to show me all that God desires of me, for me. Make my thoughts Your thoughts. My ways would be Your ways. For I choose to fix my gaze upon ALL that is above. The things of this earth void and useless. Never satisfying. But You have told me that those who hunger and thirst for righteousness shall be filled (Ephesians 4:1) and Lord I desire to be filled to overflowing. Increase my hunger that I will desire and crave more—so much more! For You have declared greatness for me, in me and through me, not of my own doing, but in and through the amazing power of Jesus Christ alone. For in Him I live, move, and have my being (Acts 17:28) and the freedom found there is glorious. Mighty. For the weapons of my/our warfare are not of the flesh but have divine power to destroy strongholds. I/We destroy arguments and every lofty opinion raised against the knowledge of God, and take every thought captive to obey Christ, being ready to punish every disobedience, when your obedience is complete (2 Corinthians 10:4-6). I will be faithful to renew my mind and to "present my body as a sacrifice—alive, holy, and pleasing to God—which is my reasonable service. (I will not) be conformed to this present world but (I will) be transformed by the renewing of my mind, so that you may test and approve what is the will of God—what is good and well-pleasing and perfect" (Romans 12:1-2 NET). I will fix my eyes on You alone Jesus and hide Your word in my heart that I may not sin against You (Psalm 119:11 NKJV). I commit this to You and pray all of this in the mighty name of Jesus. - so be it!

Day 8

Rest in God alone, O my soul, for my hope comes from Him. He alone is my rock and my salvation; He is my fortress; I will not be shaken (Psalm 62:5-6 BSB).

The sweet and rich gift of rest. The beside the still waters rest that I am assured of. You alone God lead me beside still waters (Psalm 23), and my soul is restored. Refreshed. The very peace of God flooding my soul as I have been lovingly led and my every need met. For You oh God, are my Shepherd and in You I lack nothing. Absolutely nothing do I lack. The peace that I have come to love and know is found within me, through Christ. For there is nothing that this world can ever offer that would satisfy my soul.

You alone God, are my Rock. The very foundation upon which my entire life exists. For You are the very One Who created me. Giving me great purpose. The unwavering truth of knowing that You are the Anchor that holds amidst all of life's storms. Your Word declaring that, "In this world you will have trouble," but praise be to Jesus who encouraged us with these words, "But take heart! I have overcome the world" (John 16:33 NIV).

My heart filled with abundant praise and adoration for my life is rooted and grounded in the love of God. Jesus the very Cornerstone. My life no longer like a ship tossed about aimlessly, but I live rejoicing. Knowing that I am called to seek first God's kingdom (Matthew 6:33), and it's in that sweet abiding place, the place of surrendered living, that I am satisfied. And like the woman at the well, may I ever increasingly know the Source of Your life-giving water. For Jesus said that "everyone who drinks the water that He gives will never thirst. The water becoming in me/them a spring of water welling up to eternal life" (John 4:14 NIV). May I drink deeply. May I drink often. For I know that I will never thirst again. I pray all of this in the mighty name of Jesus. - so be it!

Day 9

I am convinced and confident of this very thing, that He who has begun a good work in you will [continue to] perfect and complete it until the day of Christ Jesus [the time of His return] (Philippians 1:6 AMP).

Today, I stand in confident trust that the work You began in me Lord will see completion. From the rising of the sun, to the going down of the same, Your name Lord I will praise. Trusting Your lead all the while holding Your hand. For You hold both my hand and my heart. The journey is secure. Rich. Beautiful. For You have promised to never leave nor forsake me (Deuteronomy 31:6) and I trust You completely, confident in Your Word. Leading me to walk courageously—boldly, for Your foundation of these truths is thick and cannot be shaken. Your walls of protection are secure, safe, and impenetrable. You alone Lord, are my Strong tower. I can always run in, and I am safe (Proverbs 18:10)!

Therefore, I stand fully convinced and confident that Your finished work will be mine upon Your glorious coming. For You are my soon and coming King! I wait patiently for Your return, but choose to be active, diligent, and faithful until You do. Choosing to rejoice in "this" day, for You alone have created it. Choosing to be one of biblical integrity. Stewarding well my possessions, thoughts, time, and money. May all I set my hands to bring You glory and honor until I meet You face to face. For it will be my greatest joy to bow at Your feet and confess that truly You are the Son of the Living God! I pray all of this in the mighty name of Jesus. - so be it!

Day 10

Remember my affliction and my wanderings, the wormwood and the gall! My soul continually remembers it and is bowed down within me. But this I call to mind, and therefore I have hope: The steadfast love of the LORD never ceases, his mercies never come to an end; they are new every morning; great is your faithfulness. "The LORD is my portion," says my soul, "therefore I will hope in him" (Lamentations 3:19-24 ESV).

Great is Your faithfulness to me Lord. You have always been faithful to me even when in times I could not see it, feel it, or understand it. For You promised to never leave me. At times when life gets difficult and sometimes seemingly unbearable, I know full well that You never turn Your back. You are never at a distance. But You are faithful to love and care for me. Your steadfast love never ceases. It does not know an end (Lamentations 3:22-23). For You are love! And Your mercies? They are new every morning. All that You have ordered and purposed for me today has been greeted by Your new mercies.

Lord, You are my portion. I cannot run after another. Keep my heart and mind focused on You and You alone. For to seek another would be against that which You have asked of me. I will have no other gods before You. I truly love You with all my heart. Why would I ever desire to run into the arms of another? Your embrace is sweet, sweeter than honey. May I continually and always gaze upon Your beauty. Talking to You daily without reservation. Not bound by shame and guilt but lavishly loving You for all that You have done and for all that You are. I will rejoice always. Praying continually and I offer to You my thanksgiving and gratitude. My praise and my worship. For there is None more worthy than You. Thank you, Jesus! I pray all of this in the mighty name of Jesus. - so be it!

MAY WE BE
YOUR LOVE SONG

Days 11-20

May we now agree in prayer for us as the Church. That we will become the body of Christ as declared in the New Testament. We will be of one mind—having the mind of Christ. May our desire be all that God would have for us, His Beloved. For Christ came "so that [in turn] He might present the church to Himself in glorious splendor, without spot or wrinkle or any such thing; but that she would be holy [set apart for God] and blameless" (Ephesians 5:27 AMP). May our desire be to pursue God's call, to be Holy as He is Holy. "Because it is written, "YOU SHALL BE HOLY (set apart), FOR I AM HOLY" (1 Peter 1:16 AMP).

So much has taken place over the past 10 days as many of you have joined in agreement that you will be faithful to serve our Beloved Jesus in a worthy manner. One of devotion. Commitment. Love. Much more will be accomplished as Holy Spirit leads us into a prayer of agreement that we the Church would commit to walking in unity, in and through Christ. Joining all of Heaven, the Saints of old, in one harmonious choir singing Holy, Holy, Holy, Lord God Almighty! May we unite in sharing the Gospel and love of Jesus. Sharing the Good News that will transform their lives, restore their families and unite our churches. The world seeing the love of God in action through us, His Beloved.

So, we pray Lord, standing and declaring together, according to Ephesians 4:1-6, that we will, "live a life worthy of the calling to which you have been called [that is, to live a life that exhibits godly character, moral courage, personal integrity, and mature behavior—a life that expresses gratitude to God for your salvation], with all humility [forsaking self-righteousness], and gentleness [maintaining self-control], with patience, bearing with one another in [unselfish] love. Make every effort to keep the oneness of the Spirit in the bond of peace [each individual working together to make the whole successful]. There is one body [of believers] and one Spirit—just as you were called to one hope when called [to salvation]—one Lord, one faith, one baptism, one God and Father of us all who is [sovereign] over all and [working] through all and [living] in all" (AMP). May we walk as Christ did in all lowliness, gentleness, with longsuffering, bearing with one another in love. May we daily seek Holy Spirit's help to walk in the bond of peace continuously and faithfully. May our families, friends, co-workers, and city see Christ in us. Our Hope. Their Hope. May we as John 13:34 says, live out Christ's command of loving one another, as He loved us. May we never lose sight of Your incredible love for us Lord and may we never cease in sharing Your incredible love with others. Always and forever fulfilling Your commandment to "go into all the world and preach the gospel to every creature" (Mark 16:15 KJV). For we are Your "chosen race, a royal priesthood, a holy nation, a people for Your (His) own possession (1 Peter 2:9 ESV). May we delight in this and live according to that which You have called us. May the streets, hi-ways and bi-ways resound of Your love and unity within us Lord. Knowing that "your love for one another will prove to the world that you are my disciples" (John 13:35 NLT). May we love each other as Christ loved, willing to give of ourselves, even unto death, devoted to honouring one another and Christ in all we say and do. May we never give way to anything that would lead to the destruction of Your Beloved. May we be ever mindful to "encourage one another and build one another up (1 Thessalonians 5:11 KJV) and "speak to one another in psalms, hymns, and spiritual songs, singing and making melody in your heart to the Lord (Ephesians 5:19 NKJV). We ask all of this in the mighty name of Jesus. - so be it!

Day 11

I appeal to you, brothers, and sisters, in the name of our Lord Jesus Christ, that all of you agree with one another in what you say and that there be no divisions among you, but that you be perfectly united in mind and thought (1 Corinthians 1:10 NIV).

Father, we thank You for Your written Word that leads us into all truth. We thank You for your instruction and call to come and walk in unity. Thank You for Your gift of revelation that shows us Your ways—Your Truths. We ask Lord that You would awaken us to Your call to unity. May we lay aside anything that would stand in the way of this command. May we repent of anything that we have allowed to bring or cause division. May we offer and receive forgiveness to those to whom we have caused offense leading to division. For Your Word says in Matthew 6:15 (NLT) that if we "refuse to forgive others, You Oh Father will not forgive our sins." May we heed the work of Holy Spirit as He speaks to us about forgiveness within our own hearts. We pray that our minds and thoughts would be of one accord focused on You Lord. May we not be drawn away to gossip but found to be trustworthy (Proverbs 11:13). May we be diligent "to preserve the unity of the Spirit in the bond of peace (Ephesians 4:3). May we all "be quick to listen, slow to speak and slow to become angry because human anger does not produce the righteousness that God desires" (James 1:19. 20 NLT). May the words of my mouth and my thoughts be acceptable in your sight, O Lord, my sheltering Rock, and my Redeemer (Psalm 19:14 NET). We pray all of this in the mighty name of Jesus. - so be it!

Day 12

Blessed is the man that trusteth in Jehovah, and whose trust Jehovah is (Jeremiah 17:7 ASV).

Blessings upon blessings. These are our glorious inheritance. Thank you, Lord, for the abundant blessings that You have so beautifully bestowed upon Your children. They are many! They are great! May we never lose sight of all that You have done and given to us. The many ways and blessings that You still have for us. The kingdom You came to reveal as seen through Your Sermon on the Mount (Matthew 5). We are a blessed people for ours is the Kingdom of Heaven. You have given us great Comfort. Ours is the inheritance of earth. We are satisfied. Given to us the glorious gifts of mercy and revelation. Repentance and grace. We have been adopted and called Your sons/daughters. Us calling You Abba, Father (Romans 8:15).

Make us ever mindful that the blessings You bestow upon us are always and forevermore worthy of our praise. For "there is none like You among the gods, O Lord, nor are there any works like Yours. All the nations You have made shall come and worship before You, O Lord, and shall glorify Your name. For You are great and do wondrous things; You alone are God (Psalm 86:8-10 NKJV). We truly are a blessed people. We praise You Lord! We praise Your Holy Name! - so be it!

Day 13

Be strong and courageous. Do not fear or be in dread of them, for it is the LORD your God who goes with you. He will not leave you or forsake you" (Deuteronomy 31:6 ESV).

Lord, make us ever mindful that we are not called to walk this faith journey alone. We desperately need Your direction, counsel, and comfort—always! For we cannot face this world without You. Your very Word telling us that "in this world we will have trouble" (John 16:33 NIV). Glorious is our knowing that You also told us to "take heart!" Offering to us Your precious gift of peace. For You have already overcome the world. Our strength coming from You and You alone. May we intentionally put on the garment of praise at times when our spirit is heavy. Isaiah 61:3 says to put on "a joyous blessing instead of mourning, festive praise instead of despair" (NLT). Being clothed in the beauty of Your praise. Where our hearts and minds are set upon You and not on ourselves nor our circumstances. May we rejoice in the knowing that the "joy of the Lord is our strength" (Nehemiah 8:10 KJV). Reminding us always that You alone are the One who draws men unto Yourself. For You desire that all men would come to know You (1 Timothy 2:4-6).

Awaken within us how precious and incredible Your gift of salvation was to us. All that You did for us was/is incredible. Beautiful. Draw us away quickly from temptation that would tempt to draw us in to sin. Lead us away from the areas of complacency in our lives. May we repent from that which has kept us distant from You. Awaken within us Your call to live our lives as unto Christ in all ways. As Nehemiah encouraged the people, so too do we encourage ourselves with the truth that "the joy of the Lord is your/our strength" (Nehemiah 8:10 KJV). It is not anything in and of ourselves, but ALL that we need is found in You. Lead us into deeper commitment to all that You have for us. Walking in our glorious inheritance of praying with the Authority of Christ in us. The power of the resurrected Christ! How incredible are Your works,

Lord. We give You thanks and praise for Your revealed truth of Scripture that calls us closer to You. We thank You for the work of Holy Spirit who leads us into the knowledge and understanding of the Revealed Word of God, Christ Jesus. For we have been drawn by the power and work of the Holy Spirit. We pray with much thanksgiving for all these things in the mighty name of Jesus. - so be it!

Day 14

For this reason I bend my knees before the Father, from whom every family in heaven and on earth derives its name, that He would grant you, according to the riches of His glory, to be strengthened with power through His Spirit in the inner self, so that Christ may dwell in your hearts through faith; and that you, being rooted and grounded in love, may be able to comprehend with all the saints what is the width and length and height and depth, and to know the love of Christ which surpasses knowledge, that you may be filled to all the fullness of God. Now to Him who is able to do far more abundantly beyond all that we ask or think, according to the power that works within us, to Him be the glory in the church and in Christ Jesus to all generations forever and ever. Amen (Ephesians 3:14-21 NASB).

Father, we posture our hearts before you, bowing in love, adoration, affection, and delight. For Your name is great and greatly to be praised. For "the name of the LORD is a strong fortress; the godly run to him and are safe (Proverbs 18:10 NLT). We are never left alone but You have given us Your abiding presence in Your Holy Spirit—always. Holy Spirit power is mighty in us, and we are strengthened. We take great delight in knowing that we are rooted and grounded in Your love. Oh, how vast is Your love and yet You lavish it upon us for we were made by You to receive Your love. Our hearts are overwhelmed by the magnitude of Your love. It is vast and beautiful. May we never abuse our relationship with You. For we must never allow sin and our fleshly desires to be given any place within us, for to choose that over You would be an abuse of grace—of all that You, Jesus, did for us. You have commanded that we would not have any other gods before You, so we commit to that today—no one but YOU! Nothing else but YOU! We will not allow others, fear, shame, guilt, things, electronics, fear, time, steal away our praise today. We commit ourselves to praise today. We commit ourselves to You and You alone today. Offering our worship, our words, our thoughts. May our minds be fixed on You and You alone, the One true God. We pray all of this in the mighty name of Jesus. - so be it!

Day 15

Now we that are strong ought to bear the infirmities of the weak, and not to please ourselves. Let each one of us please his neighbor for that which is good, unto edifying. For Christ also pleased not himself; but, as it is written, the reproaches of them that reproached thee fell upon me. For whatsoever things were written aforetime were written for our learning, that through patience and through comfort of the scriptures we might have hope. Now the God of patience and of comfort grant you to be of the same mind one with another according to Christ Jesus: (Romans 15:1-5 ASV).

Lord, grant to us clarity, patience and understanding for one another. As each of us continues to persevere on their own journey of faith. May we be sensitive to those who are not as far along and be aware that there will be those ahead of us, reminding us that we are all on the same journey, our life in Christ. Make us ever mindful that we have been grafted into Christ. And from that place always comes the Fruit of Your Spirit. Love, Joy, Peace, Patience, Kindness, Goodness, Gentleness, Faithfulness and Self-control (Galatians 5:22-23 NIV). The evident work of Christ in us. For we have nothing to offer in and of ourselves, but the joy and pleasure that we have in serving You Lord with the glorious evidence of Holy Spirit within us. May our fruit be evident. Abundant. Showcasing Yourself through Your Church and our city. Bring to our remembrance often the call that "we are the Light of the World—like a city on a hilltop that cannot be hidden" (Matthew 5:14 NKJV). Forgive us when we have forgotten to shine in the dark places. Forgive us for having been taken by the world and its ways. May our hearts be captivated by You and You alone, Lord! Now, forever, and always. May our eyes never be turned away from those who need You. Teach us how to listen to Your Holy Spirit as He leads us to those who are searching for Truth. Make us bold and courageous so that we will tell others about You. May we never partner with fear, disobedience, and intimidation. These three can so easily create barriers to those who are truly searching for help, hope and love.

People need Jesus! May we victoriously shout out, "I am not ashamed of this Good News about Christ. It is the power of God at work, saving everyone who believes (Romans 1:16 NLT). But we will boldly declare of all the wonderous works You have performed in us. Our lives transformed by the power of Your Holy Spirit and the Word of God. May we walk in humility. May we remain steadfast. May we always seek after Your divine awareness—revelation to that which may hinder our walk with You. Lead us to repentance—and quickly, so that we may not have anything between ourselves and You. We pray all of this in the mighty name of Jesus. - so be it!

No Other Love

God cannot have another love. We, the Bride of Christ, are the object of His affection. He cannot leave us to go to another for "we" are the ones He created to receive His love. He cannot change His mind and give His love to another because there is no other! We are the only ones to whom His great love is intended. He cannot pursue another. There can be no adultery in Him. For to leave us would be against His promise to never leave nor forsake. For Him to pursue another would mean that our created value is void and why would He have even concerned Himself with us since the beginning of Time? In our mother's womb (Psalm 139:13)?

Oh, how deep the Father's love for us. Given to us. His incredible, indescribable, unfathomable love for me, for us, for our city. We have and will continue to be, and forevermore will be the object of His affections, time, attention and His unconditional love.

Day 16

Let us hold tightly without wavering to the hope we affirm, for God can be trusted to keep his promise (Hebrews 10:23 NLT).

How encouraging are Your words to us today, Lord. What assurance we have as we hold onto Hope, the hope found in Jesus and fullness of knowing that we can be confident in the One in whom we hold onto. We can walk in the confident knowing as the Psalmist who wrote, "Your steadfast love, O Lord, extends to the heavens, your faithfulness to the clouds. Your righteousness is like the mountains of God; your judgments are like the great deep; man and beast you save, O Lord. How precious is Your steadfast love, O God! The children of mankind take refuge in the shadow of your wings" (Psalms 36:5-7 ESV). May we as Abraham (Romans 4), deny entry to unbelief. Highlight anything that would lead us away from You and the promises that You have for us. Let us never waver concerning the promises of God. We want to grow strong in our faith so that we too will bring glory to God. Being fully convinced that God can do what He has promised (Romans 4:20). May we become fully convinced of Your unfailing love and faithfulness. May we come to know full well that You have been and will always be faithful, true, and unwavering in Your promises—for they are yes and amen! We pray all of this in the mighty name of Jesus. - so be it!

Day 17

O Lord, you alone are my hope. I have trusted you, O LORD, from childhood. Yes, you have been with me from birth; from my mother's womb you have cared for me. No wonder I am always praising you! My life is an example to many because you have been my strength and protection. That is why I can never stop praising you; I declare your glory all day long (Psalm 71:5-8 NLT).

Today, "I will praise You, for I am fearfully and wonderfully made; Marvelous are Your works, And that my soul knows very well" (Psalms 139:14 NKJV). Lord, we come and sing, making a joyful noise to the Rock of our salvation! Let us come into His presence with thanksgiving; let us make a joyful noise to Him with songs of praise! For the LORD is a great God, and a great King above all gods. In His hand are the depths of the earth; the heights of the mountains are His also. The sea is His, for He made it, and His hands formed the dry land. Oh come, let us worship and bow down; let us kneel before the LORD, our Maker! For He is our God, and we are the people of his pasture, and the sheep of His hand (Psalms 95:1-7 KJV). I give thanks to You, O Lord my God, with my whole heart, and I will glorify Your name (Psalm 86:12 NLT). May our lives be lived out as an example to many because You are our strength and protection. That is why we will never stop praising You. Our lives, a daily offering as we cannot help but dwell in Your glorious new mercy morning. Your love envelops us. Your song sung over us (Zephaniah 3:17), and Your declarations of all that we are. Your handiwork marvelous. Your gifts of revelation, salvation, transformation, all that we need, require us to be all that You have called us to be. We cannot help but give You all the honour, glory, and praise. We will both now and for evermore declare Your glory all day long (Psalms 71:8).

May our life song be declared and heard by those whom we encounter today. May they alone see Jesus. The transformative work of Christ in us. Hearing the heart of Jesus which declares love and truth over them. May we see those held captive set free today. Wayward minds, hearts and children hearing Love's call to come back home. Restore homes, even now, to receive these dear ones as they make their trek back home, today! May the love of Christ be evident in and around our city today. May the Light of Christ be seen today in Your children Lord, so that people comment that they can see a visible, evident "something" about us. Light of Christ be a beacon within our city! Dispel darkness so that those who have been held captive will shout of their freedom found in Christ. In Jesus' name. - so be it!

Day 18

Then Joshua said to them, "Do not be afraid, nor be dismayed; be strong and of good courage, for thus the LORD will do to all your enemies against whom you fight" (Joshua 10:25 NKJV).

The world can be fierce. A mighty raging battleground. The spaces/places where our enemy seeks to take us down and out. John 10:10, Jesus telling us that the enemy only comes to steal, kill, and destroy. There is no good in him. Ever "prowling around like a roaring lion, looking for someone to devour" (1 Peter 5:8 NLT). Our enemy, especially of late, seems to be gaining ground, *almost* moment by moment. Our schools, workplaces, political offices, homes, churches and streets battered by every wind and wave. But Lord, we rejoice in knowing that You did not stop with telling us about our enemy and his tactics, but You declared with much comfort and insight that we are to "fear not" for You have ALREADY overcome! We give You thanks and praise for this overcoming victory! We thank You that You did not leave us comfortless nor defenseless. You assured us that in Your leaving, Holy Spirit would come to us. And that He did! For we do not fight against flesh and blood, "but against principalities, against powers, against the rulers of the darkness of this age, against spiritual hosts of wickedness in the heavenly places (Ephesians 6:12 NKJV). Thank You Lord, that You have given us ALL we need to walk in overcoming victory over our enemy. We have all authority in Christ Jesus to take down and trample on. Thank you for the gift of the armor of God. Each piece imperative to our waring, our survival, and our overcoming victory! For we are more than conquerors in Christ Jesus (Romans 8:37). Our Victory Cry, "This is our God!" Beloved, we are not overcome, but overcomers! We are not battle worn and left defenseless, but we have been given the power to tread on serpents and scorpions, and over all the power of the enemy: and nothing shall by any means hurt you (Luke 10:19). Our victory shout? May it be as David was before Goliath, shouting, "the battle is the Lords and His hand is over us" (1 Samuel 17:47 AMP). We pray all this in the mighty name of Jesus. - so be it!

Day 19

When the perishable has been clothed with the imperishable and the mortal with immortality, then the saying that is written will come to pass: "Death has been swallowed up in victory." "Where, O Death, is your victory? Where, O Death, is your sting?" The sting of death is sin, and the power of sin is the law. But thanks be to God, who gives us the victory through our Lord Jesus Christ! Therefore, my beloved brothers, be steadfast and immovable. Always excel in the work of the Lord, because you know that your labor in the Lord is not in vain (1 Corinthians 15:54-58 BSB).

Thank You God for being such a faithful God in whom all our victory has been given and declared through all the works Your precious Son, Jesus Christ did for us. We agree together as brothers and sisters in Christ that Your love Lord knows no end. You are our steady, solid, immovable foundation upon which we stand. We thank You for the gift of Your Son upon the Cross. Such sacrifice to redeem us unto Yourself. We are humbled by Christ who gave Himself so that we would be restored to You, O God. We celebrate Christ's victory over death, hell and the grave. The overcoming resurrection power that not only brought forth victory but destroyed death. Destroying death in His rising again. How we celebrate You our Resurrected Jesus for without Your resurrection, we would have been eternally lost. But thanks be to You O God, the One who rose in triumph and victory. We are humbled by such a gift. We praise You with our words and our lives. Offering ourselves as living sacrifices. We do not live our lives in vain, rather we run into all that You have for us. May we love as Christ loved. The very giving of ourselves; the laying down of our lives. May we see others through Your eyes of compassion, grace, and mercy. May all we do be saturated in Your love. For to serve from any other place would leave us doing things of our own accord, rather, we will speak the truth in love, growing up in every way into Him who is the head, into Christ, from whom the whole body, joined and held together by every joint with which it is equipped, when each part is working properly, makes the body grow so that it builds itself up in love (Ephesians 4:15-16).

    Rejoicing we give You glory! With gladness we rejoice in You; we will sing the praises of Your name, O Most High (Psalms 9:2). Lord, we trust in Your unfailing love. Our hearts choose to rejoice in Your salvation. We choose to sing Your praises for You have been and will remain faithful now and forevermore (Psalm 13:5-6). We pray all of this in the mighty name of Jesus. - so be it!

Day 20

And now there remain: faith [abiding trust in God and His promises], hope [confident expectation of eternal salvation], love [unselfish love for others growing out of God's love for me], these three [the choicest graces]; but the greatest of these is love (1 Corinthians 13:13 AMP).

    Thank you, Lord, that we are secure in our knowing that we have faith, hope and love as true confident anchors. Given the most glorious example in Christ Jesus. We are confident in You. For we fully and completely believe the entire Word of God to be true. The Word of God speaking of Who You are and of Your precious promises. We give You thanks for Your word for it teaches us and transforms us into the likeness of Your Son, Jesus, who was fully confident in His Father's will for Him and for us. All that Jesus did was as unto You Father, confidently speaking "not my will, but thine, be done" (Luke 22:42 KJV). May we continue to grow in our understanding of Who You are so that our lives would be an incredible reflection of Christ in us. That we too would speak only of doing Your will and not our own. Walking as those fully convinced in Who You are, and who we are in You. Grant to us wisdom, knowledge and understanding for our desire is to know You more. We pray this in the mighty name of Jesus. - so be it!

JESUS YOU ARE OUR LOVE SONG

Days 21-30

Let all that I am praise the LORD. O LORD my God, how great You are! You are robed with honor and majesty. You are dressed in a robe of light. You stretch out the starry curtain of the heavens; you lay out the rafters of your home in the rain clouds. You make the clouds your chariot; you ride upon the wings of the wind. The winds are Your messengers; flames of fire are your servants (Psalm 104:1-4 NLT).

Whether we are on our knees, standing, sitting, or on our face, we must never cease worshipping Jesus. He is so worthy of all our praise. All our worship. All our honor. All our glory. All our lives. We were created for worship, to worship. What great joy and pleasure is found in worshipping our Beloved, Christ Jesus. Whether our hands are raised, we dance like David, or sing on key or not, play an instrument or not, we are ALL called to worship the King of Kings. Scripture telling us that one day every knee shall bow, and every tongue shall confess that Jesus is Lord (Philippians 2:10-11).

What an honour it is for us that we can praise Him now with our lives. Through our worship. In our words. In our thoughts. ALL of us being alive in Christ. For to be alive in Christ is to be dead to self. This is where the "abundant life" Christ promised us is forged. For we are no longer slaves to sin but are free! Free in Christ!

Today, and for the next 10 days, we will be focusing on the beauty of Jesus. Speaking and declaring to Him the wonderous works He has done for us. Declaring once again to the enemy that Jesus is Victorious! Risen over death, hell and the grave. In doing so, we collectively raise up, declare, and shout the precious work and name of Jesus Christ our Lord and Savior.

The enemy and his territories have been demolished and removed in our 20 days of prayer in our own lives, in the Church and now we advance into the next 10 days boldly declaring that Jesus is our love song. His name above any other name. The name to which every knee will one day bow both in heaven and earth (Philippians 2:9-11). Even now our tongues acknowledge Your Kingship. Jesus, You are Lord! Jesus, You are Lord! What great pleasure it is for us to know Your name and our delight to speak it—freely! It is an honor to worship You with our lives. There is nothing more precious than times with You in prayer. In Worship. In Praise. In quiet. In stillness. Jesus You are Prince of Peace, Lord of Lords, King of Kings, our Redeemer, Rescuer, Restorer, Savior, we love and adore You. Words unable to articulate the praise You are due. So today, we give You once again, our lives in complete surrender. For to abide and dwell with You brings great joy and delight to Your heart and we cannot help but praise You more and more. You are our love song!

Day 21

So, we have come to know and to believe the love that God has for us. God is love, and whoever abides in love abides in God, and God abides in him (1 John 4:16 ESV).

Thank you, Lord, for the incredible gift of revelation. Through Your Word You have called us to the knowledge of Your great love. Not only revealing it to us but showing Your love even while we were yet sinners. Demonstrating to us Your Own love toward us, in that while we were still sinners, Christ, You died for us (Romans 5:8). For "I have been crucified with Christ. It is no longer I who live, but Christ who lives in me. And the life I now live in the flesh I live by faith in the Son of God, who loved me and gave himself for me" (Galatians 2:20 ESV). No longer do we/I walk as one bound and in slavery. But we/I walk in the greatest of joy knowing that You are our love song. Christ You are all we need. But because of Your great love for us, God, who is rich in mercy, made us alive with Christ even when we were dead in transgressions—it is by grace we have been saved. For we were not saved by anything that we have done or could do, but it was Your incredible gift of salvation. "For it is by grace you (we) have been saved, through faith—and this is not from yourselves (ourselves), it is the gift of God—not by works, so that no one can boast" (Ephesians 2:8-9 NIV, brackets added). Jesus, You called us to abide in You—a sweet place of intimacy. Being together—often and always. And in our coming, our abiding, You have promised that You would abide in us. For we cannot produce anything of our own, but in You, You will produce much in and through us. May our hunger for You intensify. May our thirst for You be satisfied in our daily times together. May our times together be as sweet as honey. Rich. Filled with delight. Not just our hearts filled, but may we bring great joy and delight to Your heart today. Seeking only that of Your Kingdom (Matthew 6:33). May we never seek another love. For to love another means that You are not within me (1 John 2:15-17). May this never be said of us. You are our love song. - so be it!

Day 22

Let your unfailing love surround us, LORD, for our hope is in you alone (Psalm 33:22 NLT).

Father, Psalm 91:1 (ESV) says that "he who dwells in the shelter of the Most High will abide in the shadow of the Almighty." What a beautiful place You have given to us to retreat and abide in. A place of unmatched comfort, keeping and safety. For to be found in the "shadow of the Almighty" finds us completely covered in and by Your presence. What could separate us from You as we are found there? Nothing can separate us from the love of God. "What then shall we say to these things? If God is for us, who can be against us? He who did not spare his own Son but gave him up for us all, how will he not also with him graciously give us all things? Who shall bring any charge against God's elect? It is God who justifies. Who is to condemn? Christ Jesus is the one who died—more than that, who was raised—who is at the right hand of God, who indeed is interceding for us. Who shall separate us from the love of Christ? Shall tribulation, or distress, or persecution, or famine, or nakedness, or danger, or sword? As it is written, For Your sake we are being killed all the day long; we are regarded as sheep to be slaughtered." No, in all these things we are more than conquerors through him who loved us. For I am sure that neither death nor life, nor angels nor rulers, nor things present nor things to come, nor powers, nor height nor depth, nor anything else in all creation, will be able to separate us from the love of God in Christ Jesus our Lord" (Romans 8:31-39 ESV).

Thank you, Jesus, for the work of the cross for we are no longer separated. No longer lost. For You came to seek and save the lost. You were diligent in Your pursuit of us. May we be diligent in our pursuit of You. That we would desire to know You more. That we would not be given to other things, other people, and useless thoughts. But that all our thoughts would be on You. Our mind fixed and our hearts steadfast. We cannot pursue anything or anyone but You. There is great joy found in our abiding. For You declared that You would give us life, abundant life (John 10:10). We rejoice today in knowing that we do not merely survive here until You come again, but You have given us life in abundance until Your return. We praise You that You have given us this abundant joy filled, peace abiding, internal wellspring that does not dry up but gushes forth daily as we walk with You. We give You all the glory, honor, and praise. Even now our lips sing You songs of thanksgiving for all You have done. Jesus, truly You are our love song. - so be it!

Day 23

Then Jesus spoke to them again, saying, "I am the light of the world. He who follows Me shall not walk in darkness, but have the light of life (John 8:12 NKJV).

Thank you, Lord, for not just interrupting our darkness, but completely dispelling it and opening our eyes to Your light, Your marvelous and glorious Light. Our world was dark, void, empty and without hope until You stepped in and revealed Yourself to us. The path of life easier to navigate as we trust Your lead. Each step highlighted with the light of Your glory. We no longer walk in fear, for our steps are ordered, purposed, safe and secure. We do not struggle in our following for we know full well that Your ways are higher than ours. For You have told us that "My thoughts are not your thoughts, neither are your ways My ways, saith Jehovah. For as the heavens are higher than the earth, so are My ways higher than your ways, and My thoughts than your thoughts" (Isaiah 55:8-9 ASV).

Thank You, Lord, for not only creating and giving us a path to walk, but You have given us clear instructions in Your offering to "follow You." We cannot fall away if we remain in our following. May we, as Peter did, get out of the boat, step out in faith. Heeding Jesus' call to "Come!" Listening to His call as He says, "Take courage, it is I! Do not be afraid" (Matthew 14:27-33 AMP)! As we fix our eyes on Jesus we will not be taken by the distractions of this world, sinking and desperate for rescue. But we will be like those found in Peter's boat saying truly You are the Son of God. We will remain. Our gaze on Jesus the lover of our soul. The One to whom we daily sing our songs, declaring that "God so loved the world that He gave His one and only Son, that whoever believes in Him shall not perish but have eternal life (John 3:16 NIV). For there is no other way unto You God, but through Your precious Son, Jesus. Jesus, You are the Way, the Truth, and the Life (John 14:6). You are our delight, joy, stronghold, friend, and lover of our souls. We could never thank You enough for all that You have done, but we offer ourselves completely to You. An offering of praise. Worship. Adoration. Our lives bowed in worship King Jesus. - so be it!

Day 24

As he drew near to Jericho, a blind man was sitting by the roadside begging. And hearing a crowd going by, he inquired what this meant. They told him, "Jesus of Nazareth is passing by." And he cried out, "Jesus, Son of David, have mercy on me!" And those who were in front rebuked him, telling him to be silent. But he cried out all the more, "Son of David, have mercy on me!" And Jesus stopped and commanded him to be brought to him. And when he came near, he asked him, "What do you want me to do for you?" He said, "Lord, let me recover my sight." And Jesus said to him, "Recover your sight; your faith has made you well." And immediately he recovered his sight and followed him, glorifying God. And all the people, when they saw it, gave praise to God (Luke 18:35-43 ESV).

Oh Lord that we would cry out all the more! Jesus! Jesus! We worship You and lavish love upon You for all the amazing works You have done for us. The beatings. The ridicule. The unimaginable sacrifice on the cross of Calvary. Your giving far outweighing any offering we could ever bring. And yet, You call us unto Yourself to "Come." To abide. To be together in sweet intimacy. You made us for fellowship. Your initial call to "Come to me," we have heard and responded, but Your invitation was not just a one time, but Your invitations are daily. They are intimate, personal, and sweet. Your desire is to lavish Your love upon us. Transforming us into Your very likeness. May You increase our excitement and our understanding of these intimate moments. To spend time with You truly a most precious gift. Like the fellowship You had with Adam and Eve in the Garden of Eden, You too call us to walk and talk with You. The times and moments so sweet. Every day there is something fresh, new. It is rich. For You said that You are the bread of Life and that anyone who hungers shall be satisfied and we desire to feast daily on fresh manna from heaven. May it be said of us that we have a heart after You. - so be it!

Day 25

Now there is in Jerusalem by the Sheep Gate a pool, in Aramaic called Bethesda, which has five roofed colonnades. In these lay a multitude of invalids—blind, lame, and paralyzed. One man was there who had been an invalid for thirty-eight years. When Jesus saw him lying there and knew that he had already been there a long time, he said to him, "Do you want to be healed?" The sick man answered him, "Sir, I have no one to put me into the pool when the water is stirred up, and while I am going another steps down before me." Jesus said to him, "Get up, take up your bed, and walk." And at once the man was healed, and he took up his bed and walked (John 5:2-9 ESV).

    Lord, we thank You for the many miracles You performed while here on earth—the many times You touched, spoke to, restored, revived, returned the lost, broken, and even raised the dead. Your power and authority resonating through the streets with many being healed and even more giving testimony to Your miracle working power. Lord, we thank You for the miracles that You have worked in each of our lives. The very miracle of our lives having been rescued from the grips of hell and given the gift of restoration to God. Our sinful hearts cleansed by the work of Jesus. This most certainly is the greatest healing we have ever known. May we never cease to tell others of Your incredible work in our lives. Make us ever mindful that our love song to You is sung through our testimony, where we declare and decree the great works of Your hand and heart. May our words be sweet, swift, and sure. May we never hesitate to share Your love with others. For You have given to us the greatest miracle and gift ever known to man. Remove from us any fear or selfishness that would keep us from telling others, "Look what the Lord has done" and may we now and forevermore declare, "This is our God!" - so be it!

Day 26

I will bless the LORD Who guides me; even at night my heart instructs me. I know the LORD is always with me. I will not be shaken, for He is right beside me. No wonder my heart is glad, and I rejoice. My body rests in safety (Psalm 16:7-9 NLT).

We will bless You Lord. For You guide us—always! We are never left alone for You have promised to never leave nor forsake us (Deuteronomy 31:6). There has never been a time when we were not on Your heart and mind. For we were created by You, for You. You formed us from my mother's womb. "O LORD, You have searched me and known me. You know when I sit and when I rise; You understand my thoughts from afar. You search out my path and my lying down; You are aware of all my ways. For You formed my inmost being; You knit me together in my mother's womb. I praise You, for I am fearfully and wonderfully made. Marvelous are Your works, and I know this very well. My frame was not hidden from You when I was made in secret, when I was woven together in the depths of the earth. Your eyes saw my unformed body; all my days were written in Your book and ordained for me before one of them came to be" (Psalm 139:1-3; 13-16 BSB).

Our foundation is safe, secure, unchanging. For You alone declare that You are the same yesterday, today and forever (Hebrews 13:8). When our city, our world is wrought in chaos, we know full well that You alone God, are never changing. Your Spirit whispers Your love in our city streets. Love calls. Lord open eyes and ears to Your love, truth, and hope. As the Spirit hovered over the chaos in Genesis 1, so too does the Spirit hover over our city. Working in the hearts and lives of those who are lost, empty, hopeless. Lord, we declare that our city will be awakened by the incredible power of the Holy Spirit. We agree for divine appointments and encounters. May we be open to hear and see those whom You are drawing unto Yourself. We rejoice now in knowing that our city is going to see renewal. Your power and transformation of lives has begun to flood our streets and hope is being found on every corner through Your people—us, the Church. Use us, Lord! We agree now in the mighty name of Jesus. - so be it!

Day 27

The LORD your God in your midst, The Mighty One, will save; He will rejoice over you with gladness, He will quiet you with His love, He will rejoice over you with singing" (Zephaniah 3:17 NKJV).

We continue to take great delight in You. Our hearts are filled with thanksgiving and praise for we know that You have been faithful to Your beloved seeking, asking, knocking. The prayers of Your people are heard because You are always listening. Our faith has strengthened as our requests have been made known and heard. You are responding to us, for You said, "where two or three are gathered in My name [meeting together as My followers], I am there among them" (Matthew 18:20 AMP). City wide prayers have been engaged in and the power of agreement has caught Your attention, Your heart, and we know full well that You have drawn near—Your ear bent low. You have heard our prayers; we are confident. You have begun a good work in many lives within our city. And that which You have begun You will complete (Philippians 1:6 NKJV). Thank you, God, for all the works You have performed, will continue to perform, and have already completed within the precious lives within our city. How near and dear the lost ones are to You as You faithfully seek the one having left the 99. Thank You for Your going. Thank You for Your finding. Thank You for Your restoring. We give You all the glory, honor, and praise. - so be it!

Day 28

O LORD, the God of our ancestor Israel, may You be praised forever and ever! Yours, O LORD, is the greatness, the power, the glory, the victory, and the majesty. Everything in the heavens and on earth is Yours, O LORD, and this is Your kingdom. We adore You as the one who is over all things (1 Chronicles 29:10-13 NLT).

May our lives bring nothing but honor and praise to You today. For You are so deserving of all that we can offer, bring. May we join with the angelic hosts and sing Holy, Holy, Holy, is the Lord of Hosts. The city's atmosphere shifting as we declare with great joy that You are Great! You are all powerful! You are glorious! Victorious! Majestic! The city streets filled with hope, wonder, joy, peace, and light. Your light dispelling darkness. Captives being set free. Dazed eyes opened to Hope. Hopelessness replaced with true joy. Thank You Lord, for we know that You are more than able to do exceedingly abundantly more than this. Miracle after miracle we will see. Signs and wonders will be our portion. And we will give You alone all the glory, honor, and praise for You are worthy of it all! - so be it!

Day 29

...constantly rejoicing in hope [because of our confidence in Christ], steadfast and patient in distress, devoted to prayer [continually seeking wisdom, guidance, and strength], (Romans 12:12 AMP).

May the joy of the Lord be evident in and through us today. Rejoicing in the blessed hope that we have been given—the very confident assured foundational truth of Christ in us. It is no longer us who live, but it is Christ in us! "My old self has been crucified with Christ. It is no longer I who live, but Christ lives in me. So I live in this earthly body by trusting in the Son of God, who loved me and gave himself for me" (Galatians 2:20 NLT). What a glorious morning of celebrating You Jesus, for in You we live, move, and have our being (Acts 17:28). Our daily commitment to prayer has drawn us closer to You for we know that "blessed is the one whom You choose and bring near to You. To dwell in Your courts. (For there) We will be satisfied with the goodness of Your house, Your holy temple" (Psalm 65:4 NASB, brackets added).

We stand strengthened, confident, knowing that You will be faithful to Your promises to draw all men unto Yourself. We walk in confident assurance that You are more than able to draw them. To heal them. To restore them. To redeem them. For we have received this glorious gift ourselves. Your faithfulness has been seen repeatedly in our lives, our families, our churches, and our cities. For there has never been a time when You were not at work. For Your works are marvelous. Powerful. Glorious. And unchanging. You are the same yesterday, today and forevermore. And You will complete every good work that You began. We praise You for Your marvellous works; they are many! We praise You for the many hearts that are being drawn by You even at this moment. Hearts turned toward home. Lord, help us to be ready to receive these dear ones with celebration and thanksgiving. Teach us how to love them where You have led them. For it's Your power through the Holy Spirit that has called them out of darkness, into Your glorious Light. May we have no part in discouragement, fault finding, unacceptance and anything else that would turn them away from You. May we only and always sing and speak of Your praise. Admonishing and building one another up into ALL that You have for us. Jesus You are our love song. - so be it!

Day 30

David praised the Lord before the entire assembly: "O Lord God of our father Israel, you deserve praise forevermore! O Lord, you are great, mighty, majestic, magnificent, glorious, and sovereign over all the sky and earth! You have dominion and exalt Yourself as the ruler of all. You are the source of wealth and honor; You rule overall. You possess strength and might to magnify and give strength to all. Now, our God, we give thanks to You and praise your majestic name" (1 Chronicles 29:10-13 NET)!

    With shouts of glorious victory, we declare as David did, "Blessed are You, LORD God of Israel our father, forever and ever. Yours, LORD, is the greatness, the power, the glory, the victory, and the majesty, indeed everything that is in the heavens and on the earth; Yours is the dominion, LORD, and You exalt Yourself as head overall. Both riches and honor come from You, and You rule overall, and in Your hand is power and might; and it lies in Your hand to make great and to strengthen everyone" (1 Chronicles 29:10-12 NASB). May these declarations of Who You are resound in our hearts, minds, and city streets. Everyone seeing and hearing the declaration, "THIS IS OUR GOD!" Your dominion Lord is "from sea to sea, and from the river unto the ends of the earth (Psalm 72:8 KJV). What honor and privilege is ours to declare Your greatness in and throughout every part of our city. Our province. Our nation. For we agree together and declare that our CITY shall be saved! You alone will draw all unto Yourself. We agree together and declare that our PROVINCE shall be saved. And we agree together and declare that,

God will keep our land, Glorious and Free!
So be it!

WHAT'S NEXT?

Much has happened over the past 30 days and so we say, THANK YOU LORD! Thank you, Lord, for Your faithfulness, to Your people and to those who so desperately still need You. We know that You will continue to do the work within our city, so may we never stop seeking, asking, knocking on behalf of those whose eyes and ears remain closed. We will commit to continued prayer. To serve well. To testify well of Your goodness. Stewarding that which You have given to us from Your faithful hands.

May all of this, the 30 days of Prayer, be large steppingstones for us to leap out in faith for more. More lives. More miracles. More of You. More! More! More! May every area of our cities be inundated with Your love, power, and presence. From the rooms of City Hall to the dirty corners of our streets, may You alone God, be seen and declared. May the light of Christ dispel the darkness giving way to the wonderful, glorious hope that is only found in You Jesus. May we never lose sight of the glorious gift we have been given in the blessed hope found in Christ and the work of His cross and resurrection.

May our lives individually be given to You in our devotion to prayer, reading the Word and abiding in You alone Jesus. May we never tire of sharing His message. May we lavish His love on all those You lead us to. Serving well. Listening well. Helping well. Giving well. Honoring well. Guarding well. Telling well. Loving well. May we as Your Church, walk in unity and love. May the Church, Your Bride, be seen in all her radiant beauty. The beauty of Christ in us. May there be no offense, no tension, no gossip, no quarreling, but may Your Beloved rise in all her splendor with the world seeing Who we are in Christ, and Him alone.

May our lives collectively sing Your songs of praise, telling the world that Jesus, You are our love song. There is no other Champion to Whom we desire to raise our voice in triumphant song. We will sing and make music, flooding the air and city streets with the declaration that

You are our love song. You alone Jesus are the lover of our souls. You alone are the One who will heal, restore, and raise up our city from the ashes. We are fully confident of this for You said that You will draw all men unto Yourself (John 12:32). Lord, continue to draw them. Use us in all the ways that You have planned for us. May we ever be quick to listen, swift to move and be ever obedient to all that You have for us. We ask and commit all of these prayers to You, fully convinced that You will answer. And it's with excited anticipation we say, LORD, so be it!

YESHUA (THIS IS OUR GOD)

David praised the Lord in the presence of God's people sayin

This is our God, Father Everlasting

Power and Glory, Majesty and Splendor

Splendor belongs to You

THIS IS OUR GOD! THIS IS OUR GOD!

THIS IS OUR GOD, YES YOU ARE!

THIS IS OUR GOD! THIS IS OUR GOD!

THIS OUR GOD, YESHUA!

Carried on the wind, the Voice we know as true

All things reconciled, behold all things are new

Clothed in the light and fire in Your eyes

Fire in Your eyes

Fire & flame are Your servants. Fire and flame are Your servants. Let me be Your servant in the dawning of the day

THIS IS OUR GOD, YESHUA!

CREDITS/ENDNOTES/ETC.

HOPE STREET

Lyrics & music by (Dawn Walda/Kevin Rogers/Karen Morand/Kevin & Paula Saunders/Daniella Franz)

ALL SCRIPTURE

Biblehub.com and Biblegateway.com

KJV, NKJV, ESV, NET, ASV, BSB, Amplified, NLT, NASB

YESHUA (THIS IS OUR GOD)

Lyrics & Music by Dawn Walda/Kevin Rogers – Youtube

Manufactured by Amazon.ca
Bolton, ON